Warehouse Management in Automotive and Manufacturing Industries

Strategies for Efficiency and Excellence

Table of Contents

Chapter 1: Introduction to Warehouse Management

Warehouse management is a critical function within supply chains, especially in industries such as automotive and manufacturing, where precision, speed, and accuracy are paramount. Warehousing goes beyond the mere storage of goods; it plays a vital role in optimizing inventory, reducing lead times, and ensuring a continuous flow of materials and products. In this chapter, we'll explore the importance of warehousing in these industries, its key functions, various types of warehouses and their roles, and the unique challenges faced within automotive and manufacturing environments.

1.1 Importance of Warehousing in Automotive and Manufacturing Industries

In the automotive and manufacturing industries, warehousing is not just about storing products; it's about ensuring an uninterrupted flow of materials, maintaining quality, and optimizing resources. Here are some of the critical roles warehousing plays:

Maintaining Operational Continuity

Warehouses enable manufacturers to keep a buffer of essential materials and parts, ensuring that production lines operate smoothly without delays. The automotive industry, for example, relies on thousands of components sourced from various suppliers worldwide. Warehousing allows manufacturers to store these components and retrieve them as needed, minimizing production downtime.

Enabling Just-in-Time (JIT) Manufacturing

Many manufacturers, especially in the automotive sector, adopt a Just-in-Time approach, where materials are delivered and used as needed. Warehouses act as staging areas, ensuring that only the required amount of parts is available at the right time. This approach reduces excess inventory and helps in cutting down waste, aligning with lean manufacturing principles.

Cost Optimization

Warehousing contributes to cost savings by reducing transportation frequency, allowing manufacturers to consolidate shipments and lower transportation costs. It also provides opportunities for bulk purchasing and volume discounts on materials. A well-managed warehouse ensures that excess inventory doesn't accumulate, freeing up capital and reducing holding costs.

Risk Mitigation

Warehousing provides a buffer against supply chain disruptions, which are common in today's globalized markets. Automotive manufacturers, for instance, depend on a global network of suppliers. A warehouse that holds critical stock can prevent a production halt when there's an unexpected delay in the supply chain.

Quality Control and Compliance

Warehouses provide a controlled environment for storing materials and finished goods, protecting them from damage, deterioration, or contamination. In automotive and manufacturing, maintaining quality standards is paramount, and warehouses offer an ideal environment for conducting quality checks on incoming materials and storing them in compliance with industry standards.

1.2 Key Functions and Objectives of Warehousing

Warehouses serve several essential functions within the manufacturing and automotive sectors. These functions go beyond simple storage and aim to streamline the supply chain while enhancing operational efficiency:

Storage of Goods

The primary function of a warehouse is to store goods in a manner that is secure and organized, allowing for quick retrieval. Automotive and manufacturing warehouses often store raw materials, parts, work-in-progress, and finished products.

Inventory Management

Warehouses play a critical role in managing inventory levels and helping manufacturers track stock movements. Effective inventory management ensures that there's no understocking or overstocking, enabling manufacturers to optimize working capital. Technologies such as Warehouse Management Systems (WMS) are used to track inventory in real time, improving accuracy and reducing stock discrepancies.

Order Fulfillment and Processing

Warehouses are integral to fulfilling orders by picking, packing, and dispatching items efficiently. The automotive industry, for example, may have unique requirements for order fulfillment, such as fulfilling production line requests on demand. A well-optimized warehouse layout enables quick and accurate order processing, reducing lead times and enhancing customer satisfaction.

Value-Added Services

Warehouses in automotive and manufacturing may offer value-added services like kitting (assembling parts into ready-to-use kits), labeling, quality inspections, or repackaging. These services allow manufacturers to customize inventory based on specific production requirements, adding flexibility to the supply chain.

Quality Control and Inspection

Quality control is a significant function in warehousing, especially for automotive and manufacturing sectors where component quality impacts final product performance. Warehouses serve as checkpoints to inspect materials and components before they proceed to the next stage, ensuring compliance with industry standards.

Consolidation and Cross-Docking

Warehouses act as consolidation centers, where multiple shipments are consolidated into a single delivery, reducing transportation costs. Cross-docking, where products are transferred directly from inbound to outbound transportation, is also common in the automotive industry, especially for parts needed urgently. Cross-docking reduces handling times and keeps the flow of goods continuous.

1.3 Overview of Warehouse Types and Roles

In the automotive and manufacturing sectors, warehouses can be categorized into various types, each serving a distinct role:

Raw Material Warehouses

These warehouses store essential raw materials that are used in manufacturing processes. In automotive, for instance, raw material warehouses hold steel, aluminum, plastics, and other materials required to manufacture vehicle components. Ensuring the availability of these materials is crucial for maintaining production schedules.

Work-in-Progress (WIP) Warehouses

WIP warehouses hold partially completed goods and components that are midway through the production process. These warehouses are critical in industries with complex manufacturing processes, such as automotive, where parts are often sent to multiple facilities before assembly. WIP warehouses help manage production flow by storing intermediate products until they are ready for the next step in manufacturing.

Finished Goods Warehouses

These warehouses store fully assembled products that are ready for distribution to customers. In the automotive industry, finished goods warehouses hold complete vehicles, while in manufacturing, they may store machinery, appliances, or other products ready for delivery. Finished goods warehouses are essential for meeting customer demand and minimizing lead times.

Distribution Centers

Distribution centers serve as central hubs for the movement of goods. They are equipped to handle high volumes of inbound and outbound goods, often with cross-docking capabilities to expedite the flow of products. In automotive and manufacturing, distribution centers support just-in-time delivery by facilitating rapid distribution to assembly lines or dealers.

Cold Storage and Specialty Warehouses

Although less common in general manufacturing, specialty warehouses (e.g., cold storage) may be necessary for certain automotive and manufacturing sectors, especially those dealing with sensitive components or perishable materials that require controlled environments.

Service Parts Warehouses

In automotive, service parts warehouses are essential for holding spare parts needed for vehicle repairs and maintenance. These warehouses are strategically located to ensure parts are readily available to service centers, reducing downtime and ensuring that customers can quickly get replacements when needed.

1.4 Challenges Unique to Automotive and Manufacturing Warehousing

Warehousing in automotive and manufacturing faces unique challenges that arise from the nature of the industries, the complexity of supply chains, and the demands for efficiency and precision. Key challenges include:

High Inventory Turnover and Just-in-Time (JIT) Demands

Both automotive and manufacturing sectors often follow JIT inventory principles, where parts and materials are stored only as needed to reduce holding costs. This approach demands efficient inventory management and quick turnaround times, putting significant pressure on warehouse operations to meet JIT requirements consistently.

Complexity in Inventory Management

Automotive and manufacturing warehouses must handle a diverse range of inventory, from raw materials to small parts and large components. Additionally, inventory levels fluctuate based on production schedules, making accurate forecasting and inventory management complex but crucial.

Strict Quality and Compliance Standards

Quality control is of utmost importance in automotive and manufacturing. Warehouses are required to ensure that every part, component, and finished product meets stringent quality standards and regulatory requirements. A single defective part can cause significant production delays or recalls, making quality management a continuous challenge.

Handling of Hazardous and Sensitive Materials

Automotive and manufacturing industries often involve materials that are hazardous, such as batteries, chemicals, or flammable substances. Warehouses must comply with specific regulations for handling and storing these materials, including safety protocols, environmental regulations, and specialized equipment, adding to the operational complexity.

Need for Advanced Technology Integration

Technology is crucial to manage the complex operations in automotive and manufacturing warehousing. From warehouse management systems (WMS) to IoT-enabled tracking devices, warehouses need to stay updated with the latest technology to maintain efficiency. However, adopting these technologies requires significant investment and training, which can be a challenge for some companies.

Space Optimization and Cost Control

In manufacturing and automotive industries, efficient space utilization is critical due to the high volume and variety of parts and materials. Warehouses are tasked with maximizing available space to store inventory while minimizing costs. This often requires innovative storage solutions, such as mezzanine systems, automated storage and retrieval systems (AS/RS), or vertical storage.

Labor Management and Safety

The need for skilled labor in warehouses is growing due to the complexity of operations. Managing labor costs, ensuring efficient workforce planning, and meeting safety standards are challenging aspects of warehousing in these industries. Automated systems and robotics are helping alleviate some labor pressures, but effective workforce management remains a priority.

In summary, warehousing in the automotive and manufacturing industries is foundational to operational success. As a strategic function, warehousing ensures a continuous supply of materials and components, supports production efficiency, and reduces costs. While these industries face specific challenges—such as stringent quality standards, space optimization, and complex inventory management—advanced technology and best practices in warehouse management continue to drive improvements in efficiency and productivity.

Chapter 2: Warehouse Design and Layout for Automotive and Manufacturing

In the automotive and manufacturing industries, the design and layout of warehouses are instrumental to achieving operational efficiency, minimizing costs, and ensuring the rapid flow of materials. A well-designed warehouse layout can significantly impact productivity, reduce lead times, and optimize space utilization. This chapter will cover the principles of efficient warehouse design, how to tailor layouts to the unique needs of these industries, strategies for maximizing space utilization, and real-world case studies that demonstrate successful warehouse layouts in automotive and manufacturing settings.

2.1 Principles of Efficient Warehouse Design

The foundation of a successful warehouse layout rests on several core design principles, each intended to improve the efficiency and adaptability of the facility:

Flow Optimization

A seamless flow of goods through the warehouse is crucial for the automotive and manufacturing industries. Efficient warehouse designs prioritize unobstructed movement for receiving, storage, picking, packing, and dispatching. Creating logical pathways and zones minimizes cross-traffic, speeds up material handling, and reduces the risk of bottlenecks.

Adaptability and Flexibility

Warehouses in these industries need to accommodate changing demands. Whether new models in automotive or shifts in production volume in manufacturing, warehouse layouts must be adaptable to reorganize storage areas, adjust aisle widths, or add new sections without disrupting operations. Flexible racking systems, modular shelving, and movable workstations are often incorporated to allow for layout modifications.

Maximizing Storage Density and Accessibility

Storage density and accessibility need to be balanced carefully. High-density storage maximizes the available space, while accessibility ensures that high-demand items are easy to retrieve. This is especially important in manufacturing, where certain components may be needed frequently. Utilizing vertical storage solutions, pallet racking, and dynamic shelving systems can help optimize storage while maintaining accessibility.

Ensuring Safety and Ergonomics

Safety is a non-negotiable priority in warehouse design. Clear markings, adequate lighting, proper aisle widths, and safety barriers protect workers from accidents. In automotive and manufacturing, where heavy or potentially hazardous materials are handled, proper ergonomics also prevent injuries. Designing stations and layouts that minimize excessive bending, lifting, and repetitive movements promotes a safer work environment.

Integrating Technology and Automation

Many modern warehouses incorporate advanced technology such as automated storage and retrieval systems (AS/RS), conveyor belts, and robotics. A design that includes automation features enhances productivity by reducing manual tasks. Additionally, integrating Warehouse Management Systems (WMS) into the layout allows for real-time inventory tracking and better space utilization, as the system can dictate the optimal placement and retrieval paths.

2.2 Optimizing Layout for Automotive and Manufacturing Needs

Automotive and manufacturing warehouses have specific needs related to handling diverse inventory types and responding to high product turnover rates. Here's how layouts can be tailored to these requirements:

Dedicated Zones for Inventory Types

Different inventory types (raw materials, components, finished products) are stored in separate zones to streamline operations. In automotive, parts like engines or body panels are stored close to the assembly line to minimize retrieval times. Similarly, manufacturing warehouses often have dedicated zones for raw materials, work-in-progress (WIP), and finished goods to enhance production flow.

Minimizing Distance for High-Demand Items

Certain parts and components are frequently needed for production. Placing these items close to picking or assembly areas reduces transit times, speeds up order fulfillment, and increases productivity. Items that need regular replenishment are often stored near the dispatch area to facilitate easier handling.

Cross-Docking Areas

Cross-docking areas can improve efficiency in JIT (Just-in-Time) environments. This is particularly beneficial in automotive, where parts are needed immediately on the assembly line. Cross-docking allows items to bypass long-term storage and move directly to production, reducing storage needs and expediting the supply chain.

Flexible Racking and Storage Systems

The diversity of inventory in automotive and manufacturing requires various storage solutions. Pallet racks, cantilever racks (for bulky items like pipes and metal sheets), and mezzanine levels (for additional storage space) are commonly used. The layout must account for these storage systems to ensure that each item has a dedicated spot and is accessible when needed.

Optimal Aisle Widths and Layout Configurations

Aisle widths should balance space efficiency with operational needs. In automotive and manufacturing, wide aisles can facilitate forklift movement for heavy items, while narrow aisles maximize storage density. Common configurations include U-shaped, I-shaped, and L-shaped layouts. Each has its advantages: U-shaped layouts centralize receiving and dispatching, while I-shaped layouts create a linear flow, ideal for high-volume operations.

2.3 Space Utilization and Storage Solutions

Maximizing space utilization is essential to accommodate diverse inventory without compromising accessibility. The following storage solutions are commonly used in automotive and manufacturing warehouses:

Vertical Storage Solutions

Vertical storage is an effective way to make full use of the warehouse height. Pallet racking and mezzanine levels allow vertical stacking of goods, effectively increasing storage capacity without expanding the footprint. Automated vertical carousels are also valuable, especially for smaller, high-value parts in automotive.

Automated Storage and Retrieval Systems (AS/RS)

AS/RS systems are ideal for large warehouses with high inventory turnover. These systems automatically store and retrieve goods based on demand, minimizing human intervention. AS/RS is especially valuable in the automotive industry, where timely and precise retrieval of parts is critical for assembly lines.

Dynamic Racking Solutions

Dynamic racking systems like flow racks and push-back racks maximize space by using gravity to move items forward. Flow racks are especially useful for high-rotation items, as they ensure easy access and streamline picking. These solutions are ideal for manufacturing warehouses with parts that are frequently replenished.

Mobile Shelving Units

Mobile shelving units reduce the need for aisle space by allowing rows of shelving to move on tracks. This storage solution can be compacted or expanded based on the needs, which is useful in manufacturing warehouses with limited floor space and fluctuating inventory.

Bulk Storage and Stacking

In cases where heavy or large items like vehicle parts or machinery components are stored, bulk storage areas with floor stacking are effective. By designating specific bulk storage areas, warehouses can reduce handling complexity for oversized items and ensure these items don't interfere with more frequently accessed stock.

Storage Bins and Small Parts Shelving

Automotive warehouses often deal with small parts like screws, bolts, and fasteners. Dedicated storage bins and small parts shelving are practical for these components, keeping them organized and accessible while saving space. Bins are often color-coded or labeled for easy identification and retrieval.

2.4 Case Studies: Effective Layouts in Automotive and Manufacturing Warehouses

Examining real-world examples can offer valuable insights into effective layout strategies in automotive and manufacturing warehousing:

Case Study 1: Toyota's Kanban-Based Warehouse Layout

Toyota's warehouses employ a Kanban-based layout to support its Just-in-Time production model. By using Kanban, the warehouse layout is organized to ensure that high-demand items are available in real time. Parts are stored in zones close to the production line, enabling quick replenishment and minimizing retrieval time. Toyota's layout uses a pull-based system, where parts are only moved or restocked when needed, reducing excess inventory and optimizing space utilization.

Case Study 2: Ford's Cross-Docking and Consolidation Center

Ford's logistics strategy incorporates cross-docking and consolidation centers in its warehouse layout. For parts destined for specific production lines, Ford minimizes handling by transferring items directly from inbound to outbound areas. This cross-docking method not only reduces storage needs but also ensures that parts are readily available on production lines. Ford's layout also includes dedicated zones for bulky items and automated conveyor systems that streamline part movement across the facility.

Case Study 3: Tesla's High-Density Vertical Storage

Tesla's warehouses emphasize vertical storage to make the most of limited space. Using automated vertical carousels and high-density pallet racking, Tesla maximizes storage capacity while ensuring that high-value parts are protected and easily accessible. The layout places frequently used parts closer to production areas and utilizes AS/RS to retrieve less frequently used items quickly. Tesla's layout prioritizes efficient use of space and minimizes time spent locating and retrieving parts, supporting the fast pace of its production lines.

Case Study 4: Caterpillar's Heavy-Duty Equipment Storage

Caterpillar's manufacturing warehouses store large, heavy components, and their layout is optimized to accommodate these items. Bulk storage areas are designated for oversized equipment, while heavy-duty shelving is used for smaller, dense items. Aisle widths are specifically designed to accommodate heavy machinery, and conveyor systems are used to transport smaller components. The layout also includes multiple access points to allow forklifts easy entry and exit, which is essential for handling large items safely.

In conclusion, the design and layout of warehouses in automotive and manufacturing industries must support a highly efficient, safe, and adaptable environment. From flow optimization and space utilization to the integration of technology, every aspect of the warehouse layout is designed to align with the fast-paced demands of these industries. Case studies from major players demonstrate that an efficient layout is not a one-size-fits-all solution but a tailored approach to meet specific operational needs and challenges. Through strategic planning and the adoption of best practices, warehouses can become an integral component in maintaining the productivity and competitiveness of automotive and manufacturing operations.

Chapter 3: Inventory Management Techniques in Warehousing

Efficient inventory management is essential for the success of warehousing operations in manufacturing and automotive industries. As these industries face fluctuating demands, diverse product types, and critical supply chain timelines, effective inventory management techniques help balance supply with demand, reduce costs, and prevent stockouts. This chapter will explore the importance of inventory control, key inventory management methods, strategies for managing seasonal fluctuations, and real-world applications in the manufacturing and automotive sectors.

3.1 Importance of Inventory Control in Manufacturing and Automotive Warehouses

Inventory control plays a pivotal role in managing materials, components, and finished goods within warehouses. For manufacturing and automotive industries, where timely availability of parts is critical, inventory control ensures that the right parts are available in the right quantities at the right time.

Improving Production Efficiency and Minimizing Downtime

Manufacturing and automotive warehouses must maintain precise inventory levels to support production. If a part is unavailable due to poor inventory control, production lines may halt, leading to significant downtime and increased costs. Effective inventory control avoids such disruptions by ensuring adequate stock levels.

Reducing Holding Costs and Avoiding Excess Stock

Storing excessive inventory ties up capital and increases storage costs. Automotive components and manufacturing parts are often bulky or sensitive to environmental conditions, requiring careful handling. Inventory control techniques help keep stock levels aligned with actual demand, reducing excess stock and associated costs.

Enhancing Order Fulfillment and Customer Satisfaction

Inventory control directly impacts customer satisfaction. Timely availability of replacement parts, accessories, and products ensures that customer orders are fulfilled promptly. In automotive after-sales services, where the demand for replacement parts is high, effective inventory management helps prevent delays and maintains customer trust.

Supporting Just-in-Time (JIT) Production Models

JIT production systems depend on precise inventory control to align materials with production schedules. This approach minimizes waste and reduces unnecessary inventory holding. Effective inventory management enables warehouses to provide a continuous supply of components, supporting streamlined, lean manufacturing.

3.2 Inventory Management Methods (ABC Analysis, JIT, Cycle Counting)

Several inventory management techniques are commonly employed in manufacturing and automotive warehousing. These techniques help classify, prioritize, and manage inventory efficiently.

ABC Analysis

ABC Analysis is a method that categorizes inventory into three groups (A, B, and C) based on its value and significance:

Category A: High-value items with low volume. These components are often crucial for production and require strict monitoring to prevent stockouts.

Category B: Moderate-value items with moderate demand. Inventory levels for B items are managed carefully to balance availability and cost.

Category C: Low-value items with high volume. These items are stocked in larger quantities but require less frequent monitoring.

ABC Analysis enables warehouses to allocate resources and management efforts effectively, focusing more attention on high-value (A) items critical to production.

Just-in-Time (JIT) Inventory Management

The JIT inventory approach aligns stock levels with immediate production needs. Rather than maintaining large quantities of stock, items are ordered and delivered only when needed in the production process. This technique minimizes holding costs and reduces waste, which is especially valuable in manufacturing and automotive sectors.

JIT inventory management requires seamless coordination with suppliers, as well as reliable demand forecasting to avoid stockouts. In automotive production, where assembly lines need specific parts at specific times, JIT inventory ensures uninterrupted flow and aligns inventory with production schedules.

Cycle Counting

Cycle counting is a technique used to count portions of inventory on a rotating basis. Unlike full physical inventory counts, which require significant time and resources, cycle counting provides frequent checks on inventory accuracy.

Cycle counting typically focuses on high-value (A) items or parts with high turnover rates, helping identify discrepancies, reduce errors, and ensure accurate inventory records. In manufacturing and automotive warehouses, where inventory accuracy is crucial, cycle counting prevents discrepancies and enables real-time adjustments.

3.3 Strategies for Managing Seasonal and Fluctuating Inventory

Seasonal and fluctuating demand can create inventory challenges for automotive and manufacturing warehouses. Anticipating and managing these variations is essential to avoid overstocking or stockouts.

Demand Forecasting and Seasonal Adjustments

Accurate demand forecasting helps warehouses anticipate seasonal peaks and adjust stock levels accordingly. Advanced data analytics, historical sales data, and market trends can predict demand patterns, ensuring the warehouse has adequate stock during high-demand periods.

Flexible Storage Solutions and Temporary Warehousing

Seasonal demand often requires additional storage capacity. Warehouses can employ flexible storage solutions, such as mobile shelving or adjustable racking, to create space when demand rises. Temporary warehousing solutions, like leasing additional storage during peak seasons, are also useful for managing seasonal fluctuations without overcommitting to permanent capacity.

Safety Stock for High-Demand Periods

Maintaining safety stock ensures availability during high-demand periods or sudden fluctuations. Safety stock acts as a buffer against uncertainties in supply or demand, especially in automotive parts warehouses where seasonal demand for replacement parts may spike.

Supplier Collaboration and Lead Time Reduction

Close collaboration with suppliers helps manage fluctuating inventory levels. By sharing demand forecasts and lead-time expectations, suppliers can adjust their production schedules to meet warehouse needs. Reduced lead times and better coordination prevent stockouts during peak demand and streamline inventory replenishment processes.

3.4 Real-World Applications of Inventory Management in Manufacturing and Automotive Warehouses

Real-world examples highlight the successful implementation of inventory management techniques in these industries, showcasing their importance and impact.

Case Study: Toyota's Lean Inventory Management

Toyota is renowned for its Just-in-Time inventory system, which is the backbone of its lean manufacturing model. By implementing JIT, Toyota reduced inventory holding costs and increased efficiency. Parts are delivered to assembly lines only when needed, minimizing waste and aligning production with demand. This approach has become a benchmark for automotive manufacturers aiming to adopt lean inventory practices.

Case Study: Ford's Use of ABC Analysis for Inventory Prioritization

Ford Motor Company applies ABC Analysis to classify its vast inventory of automotive parts. By categorizing parts based on value, demand, and criticality, Ford focuses its resources on managing high-value, high-demand items while optimizing space for less critical inventory. This strategic approach ensures that essential components are always available, minimizing disruptions in production and after-sales service.

Case Study: GE's Digital Inventory Management in Manufacturing

General Electric (GE) employs digital inventory management tools, such as IoT sensors and real-time tracking, to monitor inventory across its manufacturing facilities. Real-time data allows GE to manage inventory levels accurately, predict demand fluctuations, and automate reordering processes. Digital tools have enhanced GE's inventory accuracy, minimized manual intervention, and optimized stock levels, setting an example for digital inventory management in manufacturing.

Case Study: Tesla's Strategy for Seasonal Demand Fluctuations

Tesla's production and distribution processes face seasonal fluctuations, especially around new model releases and end-of-year peaks. Tesla's warehouses utilize flexible storage solutions and strategic partnerships with suppliers to manage these demand spikes. By adjusting stock levels and utilizing temporary warehousing solutions, Tesla meets demand without overextending its permanent storage capacity.

In summary, effective inventory management in automotive and manufacturing warehouses is integral to maintaining smooth operations, reducing costs, and satisfying customer demand. Techniques like ABC Analysis, Just-in-Time inventory, and cycle counting are widely applied to classify, prioritize, and monitor stock, while strategies for handling seasonal and fluctuating demand help manage inventory levels dynamically. By adopting these practices, automotive and manufacturing warehouses can align inventory levels with production needs, maintain high levels of efficiency, and minimize operational risks.

Chapter 4: Material Handling and Storage Systems

Material handling and storage systems play a crucial role in the efficiency of warehousing operations in automotive and manufacturing industries. The selection of appropriate handling equipment and storage systems can streamline operations, reduce labor, and enhance safety. This chapter covers the types of material handling equipment, automated storage and retrieval systems (AS/RS), best practices for safe and efficient material handling, and guidelines for selecting the right storage solutions.

4.1 Types of Material Handling Equipment (AGVs, Forklifts, Conveyors, etc.)

Material handling equipment is essential in moving materials and products within warehouses. Choosing the right equipment depends on factors such as the type of goods, weight, volume, and layout of the warehouse.

Automated Guided Vehicles (AGVs)

AGVs are autonomous vehicles that transport materials around a warehouse. They follow predefined paths or use sensors and navigation systems for route guidance, making them ideal for repetitive tasks and reducing labor requirements. In automotive and manufacturing environments, AGVs are used to move heavy components like engines, body parts, and assembled products between stations or storage areas.

Forklifts

Forklifts are versatile and widely used for loading, unloading, and transporting pallets and other heavy loads. They come in various types, including counterbalance forklifts, reach trucks, and pallet jacks, each suited to specific tasks. Forklifts allow quick movement of materials and are invaluable in warehouses dealing with bulkier items, as is often the case in automotive and manufacturing industries.

Conveyors

Conveyors are automated systems that transport goods along a fixed path, ideal for high-volume warehouses with repetitive tasks. Common types include belt, roller, and chain conveyors. In manufacturing facilities, conveyors are integrated into assembly lines, allowing parts to flow smoothly from one stage to the next.

Cranes and Hoists

For handling particularly heavy or oversized items, cranes and hoists are used. These systems are beneficial in warehouses dealing with bulky automotive components and large manufacturing machinery. Overhead cranes and gantry cranes are common types that provide vertical lifting capabilities, reducing the risk of damage and enhancing safety when handling heavy loads.

Pallet Jacks and Trolleys

Pallet jacks and trolleys offer efficient solutions for moving pallets and lighter loads over short distances. They are less complex and more affordable than forklifts or AGVs, making them suitable for small warehouses or as complementary equipment in larger facilities.

4.2 Automated Storage and Retrieval Systems (AS/RS) for Automotive and Manufacturing

AS/RS are highly automated systems that allow warehouses to store and retrieve goods with minimal human intervention. These systems are particularly advantageous for automotive and manufacturing warehouses where space optimization, speed, and accuracy are critical.

Types of AS/RS

AS/RS systems are available in different configurations, each designed to meet specific storage needs. Examples include:

Unit-Load AS/RS: Ideal for handling large, heavy items like pallets or bulky automotive parts.

Mini-Load AS/RS: Used for smaller items and boxes, often for storing components or tools.

Vertical Lift Modules (VLMs): Designed to store items vertically, allowing better space utilization in height-restricted warehouses.

Benefits of AS/RS in Automotive and Manufacturing

Space Optimization: AS/RS can utilize vertical space more efficiently than traditional storage methods, freeing up floor space for other operations.

Reduced Labor Costs: Automation minimizes the need for human labor in storage and retrieval processes, saving costs and reducing errors.

Improved Accuracy and Speed: AS/RS systems are equipped with precise positioning technology, which speeds up retrieval times and reduces the risk of errors, ensuring that parts and materials are available exactly when needed.

Application in Automotive and Manufacturing

Automotive warehouses use AS/RS to store heavy components such as engines, transmissions, and body panels, while manufacturing facilities use them to manage parts inventories and tools. These systems are essential in JIT environments where minimizing retrieval times directly impacts production efficiency.

4.3 Best Practices for Safe and Efficient Material Handling

Safety and efficiency are paramount in material handling to prevent accidents, maintain productivity, and ensure smooth operations. Following best practices helps organizations protect workers, reduce handling costs, and streamline workflow.

Training and Certification

Training employees in proper material handling techniques, equipment operation, and safety protocols is essential. Forklift operators, for instance, require specific certification and training. Regular refresher training and safety drills help keep workers informed of best practices and maintain compliance with safety standards.

Ergonomics and Safety Gear

Ergonomics is essential for minimizing strain and injury risks in manual handling tasks. Providing personal protective equipment (PPE) such as gloves, safety shoes, and high-visibility vests enhances worker safety. Ergonomic aids, such as lifting devices and adjustable platforms, can further reduce the physical strain on workers, improving safety and productivity.

Preventive Maintenance for Equipment

Regular maintenance and inspections are necessary to keep equipment like forklifts, AGVs, and conveyors in good working order. Preventive maintenance reduces the likelihood of equipment failure, minimizing downtime and potential safety hazards.

Clear Aisles and Defined Traffic Flow

Ensuring that aisles are clear of obstructions and that traffic flow is well-organized reduces accidents and improves efficiency. Clear markings for pathways and designated zones for different types of equipment, such as forklifts and AGVs, help avoid collisions and streamline movement within the warehouse.

Use of Technology for Monitoring and Alerts

Many warehouses employ real-time monitoring and alert systems to track equipment locations and status, detect obstacles, and manage traffic flow. Technologies such as RFID and IoT sensors can provide alerts if equipment malfunctions or if a potential safety hazard arises, allowing immediate corrective action.

4.4 Choosing the Right Storage Systems (Pallet Racks, Shelving, Modular Systems)

Selecting an appropriate storage system is vital for maximizing space, protecting inventory, and ensuring easy access to materials. Different types of storage systems offer unique advantages based on the nature of the items stored and the specific requirements of the warehouse.

Pallet Racks

Pallet racks are one of the most common storage solutions, particularly for heavy or bulk items frequently found in automotive and manufacturing warehouses. Pallet racks come in various configurations:

Selective Racks: Provide direct access to each pallet, suitable for fast-moving items.

Drive-In/Drive-Through Racks: Allow forklifts to enter and remove pallets from within the rack structure, ideal for high-density storage of homogeneous products.

Push-Back Racks: Pallets are loaded on nested carts that move along inclined rails, optimizing space while providing quick access to stored items.

Shelving Systems

Shelving systems are commonly used for lighter items, smaller parts, and tools. They come in different types, including:

Static Shelving: Fixed units that are best suited for small, non-palletized items.

Mobile Shelving: Moveable units that maximize space by eliminating multiple aisles.

Multi-Tier Shelving: Adds vertical storage, useful for small parts inventory in automotive and manufacturing environments.

Modular Systems

Modular storage systems offer flexibility by allowing shelves, racks, and bins to be customized and adjusted based on changing storage needs. This flexibility is valuable for automotive and manufacturing warehouses with varying product sizes and quantities, enabling quick reconfiguration to meet new demands.

Vertical Storage Solutions

Vertical storage, such as vertical carousels or vertical lift modules (VLMs), utilizes vertical space for storage and retrieval, which is beneficial in space-constrained warehouses. This type of storage system is often integrated with automation for enhanced retrieval speed and accuracy.

Bins and Containers for Small Parts

Small bins and containers are used for storing parts and components. These containers are often color-coded or labeled for easy identification. Using dedicated bins for small parts in manufacturing warehouses helps maintain organization, reduces picking times, and minimizes the risk of inventory errors.

In conclusion, material handling and storage systems are critical to the efficiency and safety of warehousing operations in automotive and manufacturing industries. By selecting the right equipment and storage solutions, and adhering to best practices, warehouses can streamline operations, improve productivity, and protect their workforce. With advancements in technology and automation, material handling is continuously evolving, allowing warehouses to optimize operations and meet the demands of modern supply chains.

Chapter 5: Warehouse Operations and Process Optimization

Warehouse operations form the backbone of supply chain efficiency, directly impacting delivery speed, order accuracy, and customer satisfaction. In the automotive and manufacturing industries, smooth and streamlined warehouse operations are critical, given the complexity of the inventory and the need for high standards in product quality. This chapter will cover essential warehouse processes, lean warehousing principles, cross-docking and transshipment techniques, and the importance of quality control in warehouse operations.

5.1 Key Warehouse Processes: Receiving, Put-Away, Picking, Packing, and Shipping

Each process within the warehouse has a specific role that contributes to the overall effectiveness and speed of the supply chain. By optimizing these processes, warehouses can enhance productivity, reduce errors, and ensure the timely movement of goods.

Receiving

The receiving process is the first step where inbound goods are verified, unloaded, and inspected for quality. In automotive and manufacturing industries, accurate receiving ensures that the right parts or raw materials are received in proper condition, reducing production delays and returns. Digital solutions, like RFID and barcode scanning, streamline receiving by quickly capturing data and identifying discrepancies between received and ordered quantities.

Put-Away

Put-away involves moving goods from the receiving area to designated storage locations. Effective put-away strategies, such as assigning high-demand items to easily accessible locations, improve retrieval times and warehouse space utilization. In automotive warehouses, where parts can vary in size and weight, optimized put-away can reduce handling time and enhance space usage.

Picking

Picking is one of the most labor-intensive and costly processes in warehousing. It involves selecting items from storage locations to fulfill orders. Picking efficiency can be enhanced by strategies such as batch picking (grouping similar orders), zone picking (assigning specific areas to workers), or wave picking (organizing picking in waves based on order priorities). In automotive and manufacturing warehouses, efficient picking is crucial, as incorrect parts or delays can disrupt production lines.

Packing

Packing ensures that items are securely prepared for transportation, minimizing the risk of damage. Proper packing requires appropriate materials and labeling to ensure compliance with handling and regulatory requirements. In automotive warehousing, where parts may be fragile or bulky, using the right packing materials is essential to avoid damage during shipping.

Shipping

The shipping process prepares completed orders for dispatch to customers or other facilities. This process includes loading goods onto transport vehicles, ensuring that correct documentation is included, and tracking the shipment. For automotive and manufacturing warehouses, timely shipping is critical to meet production schedules, as delays can result in significant downtime in the supply chain.

5.2 Lean Warehousing Principles for Process Efficiency

Lean warehousing aims to eliminate waste, enhance productivity, and streamline processes to deliver higher value with fewer resources. Lean principles are essential in industries where just-in-time (JIT) inventory and high efficiency are necessary.

Eliminate Waste

Lean warehousing focuses on eliminating the seven types of waste—overproduction, waiting, excess inventory, motion, transportation, rework, and over-processing. For instance, reducing excess inventory ensures that only necessary parts are stocked, freeing up valuable space for other operations.

5S for Warehouse Organization

The 5S method (Sort, Set in order, Shine, Standardize, Sustain) is fundamental to creating an organized, safe, and efficient workspace. In warehouses, 5S helps reduce search time, minimizes errors, and maintains cleanliness. Applying 5S principles ensures that parts, tools, and equipment are stored properly and are easily accessible.

Continuous Improvement (Kaizen)

Lean warehousing embraces continuous improvement (Kaizen), where employees are encouraged to identify areas for improvement and make small, incremental changes. In automotive and manufacturing warehouses, Kaizen can lead to innovations that streamline processes, such as implementing better picking methods or reducing the steps required in receiving and put-away.

Value Stream Mapping (VSM)

VSM is a lean tool that maps the current state of warehouse processes to identify inefficiencies and develop an optimized future state. By analyzing each step in the process, automotive and manufacturing warehouses can pinpoint bottlenecks, unnecessary steps, or delays that impact efficiency.

Standardized Work

Standardizing processes, from receiving to shipping, ensures consistency and quality across all warehouse functions. For example, standardizing the put-away process by defining specific storage locations based on demand frequency can improve efficiency and accuracy, reducing delays and errors in order fulfillment.

5.3 Cross-Docking and Transshipment Techniques

Cross-docking and transshipment are warehousing strategies that enhance speed and efficiency by reducing or eliminating storage time. These techniques are particularly beneficial in environments where inventory turnover needs to be quick to meet production demands.

Cross-Docking

Cross-docking is a technique where inbound goods are directly transferred to outbound shipments, bypassing the need for storage. This approach is useful in JIT environments, like automotive manufacturing, where materials are delivered just before they're needed on the production line. Cross-docking reduces inventory holding costs, minimizes storage needs, and accelerates delivery times. For example, a manufacturer may receive parts from multiple suppliers, consolidate them at a cross-docking facility, and send them directly to assembly plants.

Transshipment

Transshipment involves temporarily holding goods before transferring them to different destinations or transport modes. Unlike cross-docking, transshipment may include short-term storage to consolidate shipments or change transportation methods. In automotive and manufacturing industries, transshipment is helpful when coordinating multiple suppliers or managing complex supply routes.

Benefits of Cross-Docking and Transshipment

Reduced Inventory Levels: Both techniques minimize storage needs, allowing warehouses to maintain leaner inventory.

Faster Delivery Times: By avoiding storage, products reach end destinations faster, essential for time-sensitive industries like automotive.

Cost Savings: Lower inventory and storage requirements translate into reduced holding costs, contributing to cost-effective operations.

Challenges and Considerations

Coordination: Cross-docking and transshipment require precise timing and coordination among suppliers, carriers, and warehousing teams.

Limited Flexibility: Cross-docking works best when there is a steady demand for items, which can be challenging in industries with fluctuating needs or variable production schedules.

5.4 Quality Control in Warehouse Operations

Quality control in warehouse operations is essential for maintaining product integrity, ensuring customer satisfaction, and reducing costs associated with errors or returns. By implementing rigorous quality control processes, warehouses can uphold high standards in handling, storing, and shipping inventory.

Inbound Quality Checks

Conducting quality inspections during receiving ensures that only defect-free materials enter the warehouse. For automotive and manufacturing warehouses, this step is crucial, as defective parts can lead to production delays, costly recalls, or compromised safety.

In-Process Quality Control

Regular inspections during picking, packing, and storage help identify potential issues before items are shipped. Quality checks can be as simple as verifying pick lists or conducting visual inspections of packaged items to ensure they meet standards. This process is particularly useful in high-value industries like automotive, where parts must meet strict specifications.

Compliance and Documentation

Maintaining detailed documentation of quality checks and compliance protocols helps warehouses trace issues back to their source and adhere to industry standards. Documentation is especially important in regulated industries, where audits are common. For instance, automotive warehouses need records for quality checks on critical parts, from receipt to shipping.

Employee Training and Awareness

Training employees on quality control protocols enhances their ability to detect and address issues before they escalate. Employees who understand the importance of quality and know what to look for can help prevent errors, reduce waste, and improve overall warehouse performance.

Using Technology for Quality Control

Technology, such as RFID, barcode scanning, and IoT sensors, plays a significant role in quality control. These tools help track product movements, monitor conditions (e.g., temperature and humidity), and ensure that inventory complies with quality standards. In the automotive sector, RFID tags can provide real-time tracking of parts, ensuring traceability and reducing the risk of errors in assembly.

Warehouse operations in the automotive and manufacturing industries require precision, efficiency, and adherence to high standards. By optimizing processes, implementing lean principles, leveraging cross-docking and transshipment techniques, and maintaining rigorous quality control, warehouses can meet the demanding needs of these sectors. Process optimization not only reduces costs but also ensures timely and accurate delivery of components and products, helping manufacturers achieve their goals and maintain a competitive edge in the market.

Chapter 6: Technology and Automation in Warehousing

Advancements in technology have transformed warehousing, bringing unprecedented levels of automation, data accuracy, and process efficiency. For the automotive and manufacturing industries, these innovations help manage complex supply chains and streamline operations to keep pace with growing demand and evolving customer expectations. This chapter covers the role of Warehouse Management Systems (WMS), the integration of IoT, AI, and robotics, the benefits and challenges of warehouse automation, and future trends in warehouse technology.

6.1 Role of Warehouse Management Systems (WMS) in Automotive and Manufacturing

A Warehouse Management System (WMS) is a software solution designed to support daily warehouse operations by tracking inventory, managing orders, and streamlining processes such as receiving, put-away, picking, and shipping. In the automotive and manufacturing sectors, a WMS is essential for managing high-value, high-volume inventory and ensuring efficient movement of parts and materials through the supply chain.

Inventory Tracking and Accuracy

In industries like automotive, where precise inventory levels are critical, WMS enhances accuracy by tracking stock in real-time. With barcode scanning, RFID, and automated data collection, a WMS can provide a clear view of inventory, reducing the risk of shortages or excesses and helping warehouses maintain optimal stock levels.

Order Fulfillment Efficiency

WMS streamlines order processing by optimizing picking routes, managing workloads, and ensuring that orders are fulfilled accurately and promptly. By reducing order cycle time, WMS plays a vital role in keeping manufacturing and assembly lines running smoothly.

Labor Management

WMS includes tools for labor management, such as workload tracking, performance measurement, and resource allocation. By providing insights into labor utilization, WMS enables managers to optimize staffing, which is especially valuable in the automotive industry, where labor costs can significantly impact profitability.

Automated Replenishment

For production-dependent industries like automotive and manufacturing, stockouts can halt operations. WMS can automate replenishment by setting inventory thresholds and generating purchase orders when stock levels drop, ensuring the availability of critical components.

Data and Analytics

WMS generates data on various operational aspects, from inventory turnover to order accuracy, providing valuable insights for continuous improvement. Analytics tools in WMS help managers identify inefficiencies, predict future needs, and make data-driven decisions to improve warehouse performance.

6.2 Integration of IoT, AI, and Robotics in Warehouse Operations

Integrating IoT, AI, and robotics is revolutionizing warehouse operations, enabling facilities to become smarter, more agile, and increasingly automated. In the automotive and manufacturing sectors, where precision and efficiency are paramount, these technologies are essential.

Internet of Things (IoT)

IoT connects devices, sensors, and systems within the warehouse, enabling real-time data sharing and control. IoT applications in warehouses include temperature monitoring, asset tracking, and equipment status updates. For instance, sensors can monitor conditions for sensitive automotive parts, alerting managers if temperature or humidity goes beyond acceptable ranges. IoT improves asset visibility, reduces maintenance costs, and enhances inventory accuracy.

Artificial Intelligence (AI)

AI supports predictive analytics, demand forecasting, and optimized decision-making. In warehouses, AI algorithms analyze historical data to predict demand and plan inventory levels accordingly, helping avoid stockouts or overstocking. AI-powered automation solutions can also enhance route optimization, helping pickers navigate the warehouse more efficiently and reducing travel time.

Robotics

Robots play a significant role in material handling, order picking, and packing processes. Autonomous Mobile Robots (AMRs) and Automated Guided Vehicles (AGVs) handle repetitive tasks like transporting parts and products across the warehouse. Robots can work continuously, reduce human error, and increase throughput, helping automotive and manufacturing warehouses meet demand without compromising quality.

Machine Learning and Computer Vision

Machine learning algorithms analyze patterns in warehouse data, detecting anomalies and optimizing workflows. Computer vision, combined with AI, enables automated quality control by identifying defects, damage, or discrepancies in parts and materials. In the automotive industry, this technology is invaluable, as defects in components can lead to safety issues and recalls.

Collaborative Robotics (Cobots)

Cobots are designed to work alongside humans, assisting with tasks that are too physically demanding or repetitive. Cobots can help employees lift heavy items, transport materials, or perform quality checks, improving productivity and workplace safety.

6.3 Benefits and Challenges of Warehouse Automation

Warehouse automation offers substantial benefits but also presents certain challenges, particularly in complex environments like automotive and manufacturing warehouses.

Benefits of Warehouse Automation

Increased Efficiency and Productivity: Automation reduces manual effort, speeds up processes, and increases throughput. For instance, robotic picking systems can operate faster than human pickers and work continuously, improving order fulfillment times.

Improved Accuracy: Automated systems minimize errors in picking, packing, and inventory tracking. This is crucial in automotive warehouses, where accuracy in part numbers, specifications, and quality standards is essential.

Enhanced Safety: Robots and automation reduce the need for manual handling, minimizing the risk of injuries associated with heavy lifting or repetitive motions.

Cost Savings: By optimizing labor and improving efficiency, automation can reduce operational costs. While the initial investment may be high, the long-term savings in labor, errors, and time often make it worthwhile.

Challenges of Warehouse Automation

High Initial Investment: The cost of acquiring and implementing automation technology, such as robotics and AI systems, can be substantial. This high initial investment is often a barrier for many warehouses, particularly smaller facilities.

System Integration: Integrating new automation technology with existing systems, such as ERP and WMS, can be complex and require significant IT support.

Skill Requirements: Operating and maintaining automated systems requires specialized knowledge, creating a need for skilled personnel. Warehouses may need to invest in employee training and hiring skilled technicians.

Adaptability: Automation systems are generally designed for specific tasks. Changes in demand, product type, or order profiles may require modifications to automated systems, which can be challenging and costly.

6.4 Future Trends in Warehouse Technology for Automotive and Manufacturing

The future of warehouse technology promises even more advanced and efficient solutions, driven by ongoing advancements in digitalization, automation, and AI.

Digital Twins and Simulation

Digital twins are virtual models of physical warehouses that enable real-time monitoring, simulation, and optimization of warehouse operations. In automotive and manufacturing, digital twins allow managers to visualize workflows, predict bottlenecks, and experiment with layout changes without disrupting actual operations.

5G Connectivity

The rollout of 5G technology enables faster and more reliable communication between IoT devices, robots, and management systems. In large warehouses, 5G provides the speed and connectivity needed for real-time data transmission and monitoring, enhancing automation and IoT effectiveness.

Advanced Robotics and Human-Robot Collaboration

Robotics continues to evolve, with future developments including more sophisticated, flexible robots capable of handling a broader range of tasks. Collaborative robots, or cobots, are expected to become more prevalent, allowing for safer and more effective human-robot interaction, especially in labor-intensive environments like automotive warehousing.

Edge Computing for Real-Time Analytics

Edge computing brings data processing closer to the source of data collection, such as sensors or robots within the warehouse. By processing data on-site rather than sending it to a central server, edge computing enables faster response times and real-time decision-making. In the fast-paced automotive industry, edge computing can facilitate instant adjustments in inventory management, quality control, and order processing.

Augmented Reality (AR) for Enhanced Productivity

AR technology, when combined with wearable devices, can guide warehouse workers through tasks, such as picking or inventory checks. In automotive warehouses, AR glasses could display picking routes, product locations, or assembly instructions directly in the worker's field of vision, reducing search time and minimizing errors.

Blockchain for Improved Supply Chain Transparency

Blockchain technology is emerging as a solution for tracking and verifying parts and products as they move through the supply chain. For automotive manufacturers who source parts globally, blockchain can provide a secure and transparent way to track component origins, ensuring quality and compliance throughout the supply chain.

AI-Driven Predictive Maintenance

Predictive maintenance leverages AI to analyze data from sensors on equipment, predicting when maintenance should be performed to prevent breakdowns. This proactive approach is especially valuable in warehouses with heavy equipment, such as forklifts or conveyors, as it reduces downtime and maintenance costs.

Technology and automation in warehousing are reshaping how the automotive and manufacturing sectors operate, offering tools that improve efficiency, accuracy, and adaptability. As advancements continue, these industries will see even greater reliance on digital and automated solutions, with the potential to optimize every aspect of warehouse management. Embracing these innovations will be essential for companies looking to maintain a competitive edge in an increasingly complex supply chain landscape.

Chapter 7: Workforce Management in Warehouses

Effective workforce management is crucial for the smooth operation of warehouses, particularly in the automotive and manufacturing industries, where specialized skills and adherence to safety protocols are essential. This chapter explores the strategies for hiring and training warehouse staff for specialized roles, workforce planning and optimization for peak times, ensuring safety and compliance in warehouse operations, and approaches for motivating and retaining skilled personnel.

7.1 Hiring and Training Warehouse Staff for Specialized Roles

Hiring the right people with the necessary skills and expertise is the foundation of effective warehouse management. Given the complexities of the automotive and manufacturing sectors, it's essential to have specialized roles, each requiring different competencies. Key strategies for successful hiring and training include:

Defining Job Roles and Skill Requirements

In automotive and manufacturing warehouses, roles often range from material handlers and forklift operators to quality control inspectors and inventory specialists. Each role should have clearly defined requirements, including technical skills, experience with specific equipment, and familiarity with industry regulations. This allows for targeted recruitment that aligns with the warehouse's needs.

Screening and Selecting Candidates

Assessing candidates for technical skills, attention to detail, and problem-solving ability is crucial. For instance, forklift operators should have proper certifications, while inventory specialists need experience with Warehouse Management Systems (WMS). Effective selection processes, including practical assessments and behavioral interviews, can help identify candidates best suited for the job's demands.

Comprehensive Training Programs

Once hired, employees should undergo training programs tailored to their roles. Training may include equipment operation, safety protocols, and software usage. In manufacturing warehouses, cross-training (training employees to perform multiple roles) is also beneficial, as it builds a versatile workforce that can adapt to fluctuations in demand.

Onboarding and Continuous Skill Development

Effective onboarding familiarizes new hires with the warehouse's operations, safety practices, and workflow expectations. Additionally, ongoing skill development, such as regular refreshers on safety practices or training on new technology, is essential to maintaining high levels of competence and adaptability.

7.2 Workforce Planning and Optimization for Peak Times

In industries with fluctuating demand, workforce planning is critical for handling peak times efficiently without overburdening staff or compromising on service quality.

Analyzing Seasonal Demand and Forecasting

The automotive and manufacturing industries often experience seasonal or cyclical demand. Accurate demand forecasting allows managers to prepare for peak periods, ensuring enough labor is available without excess costs during slower times. Planning based on historical data, industry trends, and customer orders can guide decisions on staffing levels.

Flexible Workforce Strategies

Maintaining a mix of full-time, part-time, and temporary employees provides flexibility. During peak times, temporary hires can supplement the regular workforce. Cross-training also supports flexibility, as trained employees can shift roles as needed to manage increased workloads effectively.

Automating Workforce Management Processes

Workforce management software can automate scheduling and optimize staffing. By analyzing real-time data on workloads, this software can dynamically adjust schedules, shift allocations, and labor assignments based on warehouse needs, ensuring optimal labor utilization and reducing overtime costs.

Efficient Shift Scheduling and Break Management

Rotating shifts and implementing efficient break schedules prevent fatigue and maintain productivity. During high-demand periods, staggered breaks can help keep operations running smoothly. Managers should also ensure adequate staffing levels to avoid burnout and excessive overtime, which can negatively impact productivity and employee morale.

7.3 Safety and Compliance in Warehouse Operations

Safety and compliance are paramount in any warehouse but are particularly critical in the automotive and manufacturing sectors, where heavy machinery and complex materials handling are commonplace. A proactive approach to safety helps prevent accidents, ensures regulatory compliance, and fosters a culture of caution and awareness.

Establishing Safety Protocols and Standards

Clear safety protocols tailored to warehouse operations are essential. This includes guidelines for handling hazardous materials, operating heavy equipment, and safe lifting practices. Employees should have easy access to these protocols and undergo regular training to reinforce safety measures.

Compliance with Industry Regulations

Warehouses must comply with OSHA (Occupational Safety and Health Administration) standards and industry-specific regulations. In automotive and manufacturing environments, this often involves standards for equipment safety, fire prevention, and handling of specific materials. Compliance with these standards helps reduce liability, maintain employee well-being, and protect the company's reputation.

Implementing Safety Training Programs

Safety training should be comprehensive, covering emergency procedures, equipment operation, and hazard recognition. Hands-on training, such as operating forklifts or navigating automated systems, is often necessary. Conducting regular safety drills and revisiting safety protocols at scheduled intervals can reinforce a culture of vigilance.

Conducting Regular Safety Audits and Inspections

Routine safety inspections identify potential hazards, ensuring that equipment is in good condition and that safety practices are being followed. Audits also assess compliance with regulatory standards and internal policies. Promptly addressing any identified safety issues is critical to preventing accidents and maintaining a safe work environment.

Creating an Open Safety Reporting System

Encouraging employees to report hazards or unsafe practices without fear of retaliation fosters a proactive safety culture. An open reporting system, whether through suggestion boxes, digital platforms, or direct communication channels, enables early identification and resolution of potential risks.

7.4 Motivating and Retaining Skilled Warehouse Personnel

Retaining skilled personnel is essential for warehouse efficiency and reducing turnover-related costs. Motivated employees are more engaged, perform better, and contribute positively to the work environment. Effective strategies for motivation and retention include:

Competitive Compensation and Benefits

Offering competitive wages and comprehensive benefits, such as healthcare, retirement plans, and paid time off, can significantly impact retention. Additional incentives, such as performance-based bonuses or allowances for night shifts, show employees that their efforts are valued and rewarded.

Career Advancement Opportunities

Providing opportunities for career growth and skill development motivates employees to stay. This could include pathways for promotion, access to specialized training programs, or the chance to take on more responsibility. For instance, experienced employees might move into supervisory roles or participate in training programs for warehouse technology.

Positive Work Environment and Recognition

A positive work culture fosters teamwork and employee satisfaction. Recognizing individual achievements, whether through "Employee of the Month" programs, awards for punctuality, or acknowledgment of exceptional performance, boosts morale and encourages continued dedication.

Providing Adequate Tools and Resources

Ensuring employees have access to well-maintained equipment, user-friendly technology, and sufficient resources is essential. Investing in quality tools and technology not only enhances productivity but also shows employees that the company is committed to providing a safe and efficient work environment.

Work-Life Balance and Flexibility

Maintaining a work-life balance is important for employee well-being and satisfaction. Warehouses can support this by offering flexible scheduling, accommodating personal requests when possible, and encouraging time-off when workloads allow. Maintaining work-life balance helps prevent burnout and supports long-term retention.

Employee Engagement Programs

Engagement initiatives, such as regular feedback sessions, team-building activities, or wellness programs, contribute to a cohesive and motivated workforce. Encouraging employee input on workplace decisions, even in small ways, can make them feel valued and involved in the warehouse's success.

Workforce management is a complex yet crucial element of warehouse operations in the automotive and manufacturing industries. By hiring qualified staff, optimizing workforce planning, prioritizing safety, and implementing strategies to retain skilled employees, warehouses can create an efficient, safe, and productive environment. Managing the workforce effectively not only ensures smooth day-to-day operations but also enhances long-term stability and adaptability, which are essential for meeting the challenges of modern warehousing.

Chapter 8: Warehouse Safety and Security

Warehouse safety and security are critical, particularly in the automotive and manufacturing industries, where the presence of heavy equipment, hazardous materials, and high-value items pose unique risks. Ensuring a safe and secure environment protects both personnel and inventory, reduces costly incidents, and complies with industry regulations. This chapter will discuss common hazards and risks in these warehouses, methods for implementing safety standards, security measures to prevent theft and unauthorized access, and the importance of emergency preparedness.

8.1 Common Hazards and Risks in Automotive and Manufacturing Warehouses

In automotive and manufacturing warehouses, hazards can arise from a variety of sources, including machinery, chemicals, and manual handling tasks. Identifying and addressing these risks is the first step toward creating a safe work environment.

Machinery and Equipment Hazards

Heavy machinery, such as forklifts, automated guided vehicles (AGVs), and conveyors, are essential in warehousing but pose significant risks if not operated safely. Improperly maintained equipment, lack of operator training, and insufficient safety protocols can lead to serious injuries. Ensuring that machinery is regularly inspected, operators are well-trained, and safety barriers are in place can mitigate these risks.

Hazardous Materials

Automotive and manufacturing warehouses often store hazardous materials, such as oils, paints, and chemicals.

Without proper handling and storage, these materials can cause fires, chemical spills, or toxic exposure. Storing hazardous materials in designated areas, using proper labeling, and equipping staff with protective gear are essential measures to ensure safety.

Manual Handling and Ergonomic Risks

Workers frequently lift, carry, and move heavy items, increasing the risk of musculoskeletal injuries. Poor ergonomic practices or lack of lifting equipment can exacerbate these risks. Providing proper training on manual handling, using mechanical aids (like pallet jacks and ergonomic tools), and designing workflows to reduce repetitive strain can help prevent injuries.

Slip, Trip, and Fall Hazards

Cluttered aisles, wet floors, and uneven surfaces are common sources of slips, trips, and falls. These incidents are preventable through regular housekeeping practices, marking hazard zones, and enforcing policies to keep pathways clear.

Electrical and Fire Hazards

The presence of electrical machinery and flammable materials increases the risk of fires. Regular electrical inspections, installation of fire extinguishers, and clear evacuation routes are essential. Fire suppression systems, along with staff training in fire response, are also crucial components of warehouse safety.

8.2 Implementing Safety Standards (OSHA, ISO) and Best Practices

Adhering to industry-recognized safety standards, such as OSHA and ISO, not only ensures regulatory compliance but also promotes a culture of safety within the warehouse.

OSHA Standards

The Occupational Safety and Health Administration (OSHA) provides guidelines for various aspects of workplace safety, including equipment operation, hazardous material handling, and personal protective equipment (PPE). Warehouses in the U.S. are required to comply with OSHA standards, which include mandatory safety training, record-keeping, and reporting of workplace incidents.

ISO Standards

The International Organization for Standardization (ISO) has established standards like ISO 45001, which focuses on occupational health and safety. ISO 45001 offers a framework for proactively managing health and safety risks. Adopting ISO standards can enhance safety practices, build employee trust, and improve operational efficiency.

Best Practices in Safety Implementation

Conducting Risk Assessments: Regular risk assessments help identify potential hazards before they result in incidents. Involving employees in risk assessments can provide insights into hidden risks.

Employee Training: Continuous training on safety protocols, proper equipment handling, and emergency response procedures reinforces safe practices.

Use of PPE: Enforcing the use of PPE, such as gloves, goggles, and high-visibility vests, helps protect employees from exposure to hazards.

Regular Safety Audits and Inspections: Scheduled audits and inspections ensure that safety measures are up-to-date and that any potential hazards are addressed promptly.

Creating a Safety Culture: Encouraging employees to report hazards and participate in safety discussions fosters a culture where safety is a shared responsibility.

8.3 Security Measures (CCTV, Access Control) and Theft Prevention

Warehouses often store valuable items, making them potential targets for theft. Implementing robust security measures is crucial to prevent unauthorized access, loss, and theft.

Closed-Circuit Television (CCTV)

CCTV cameras provide real-time surveillance and deter theft by monitoring key areas of the warehouse, such as entrances, exits, loading docks, and high-value storage zones. Integrating CCTV with motion sensors and alerts enhances security by enabling prompt responses to suspicious activities.

Access Control Systems

Access control systems, such as keycards, biometric scanners, and PIN entry, restrict entry to authorized personnel only.

Access control can be particularly useful for sensitive areas, like storage rooms for high-value items or hazardous materials. By tracking entry and exit times, these systems also help monitor employee movements and maintain records for security audits.

Alarm Systems and Motion Detectors

Alarm systems and motion detectors can detect unauthorized movements and alert security personnel. This is especially important in areas where valuable inventory is stored, as alarms can quickly notify warehouse managers of potential breaches.

Inventory Management and Tracking

Effective inventory management systems reduce the risk of internal theft by keeping track of inventory levels in real-time. Barcode scanning, RFID tags, and regular inventory audits make it easier to detect discrepancies and prevent losses.

Employee Screening and Background Checks

Conducting background checks during the hiring process can help reduce the likelihood of internal theft. Additionally, implementing policies for reporting suspicious behavior promotes accountability among employees.

Theft Prevention Training

Training employees on theft prevention protocols, such as identifying unauthorized access or suspicious behavior, can reduce the risk of theft. Creating an environment where employees feel comfortable reporting issues without fear of retribution contributes to an effective theft prevention program.

8.4 Emergency Preparedness and Response Plans

Preparedness for emergencies, such as fires, chemical spills, or natural disasters, is essential for minimizing damage and ensuring employee safety. A well-defined emergency response plan allows warehouses to respond effectively to unexpected events.

Developing an Emergency Response Plan

An emergency response plan outlines actions for different types of emergencies, such as evacuations, fire responses, and medical incidents. The plan should include clear instructions, designated assembly points, and assigned roles for employees.

Conducting Drills and Simulations

Regular drills, such as fire and evacuation drills, familiarize employees with emergency procedures, helping them react quickly and calmly during real emergencies. Simulations of various scenarios, like chemical spills or security breaches, prepare staff for different types of incidents.

Installing Emergency Equipment

Fire extinguishers, first-aid kits, and eye-wash stations should be strategically placed throughout the warehouse, especially in high-risk areas. Employees should be trained to use this equipment effectively, and regular maintenance ensures that it's in working condition when needed.

Emergency Communication Systems

Clear and reliable communication is essential during emergencies. Public address (PA) systems, alarms, and mobile alerts enable warehouse managers to quickly communicate with staff. Designating emergency contacts within the warehouse also facilitates effective coordination.

Collaboration with Local Authorities

Partnering with local emergency services, such as fire departments and medical responders, enhances preparedness. Regular site visits by local authorities can help familiarize them with the layout and potential hazards, improving response times during an emergency.

Post-Incident Evaluation

After any emergency, a post-incident evaluation should be conducted to identify what went well and where improvements can be made. This feedback loop ensures continuous improvement in emergency response planning and prepares the warehouse for future incidents.

Maintaining safety and security in automotive and manufacturing warehouses requires a proactive approach, involving regular hazard assessments, adherence to safety standards, implementation of security protocols, and well-planned emergency responses. By prioritizing safety and security, warehouses not only protect their employees and assets but also enhance overall efficiency and operational stability. The investments made in safety training, security measures, and emergency preparedness create a resilient workplace capable of handling industry-specific risks and contributing to the long-term success of the organization.

Chapter 9: Sustainable Warehousing Practices

Sustainability has become a key focus in warehousing as industries recognize the importance of reducing environmental impact and promoting eco-friendly practices. In automotive and manufacturing, where warehouses consume significant energy and resources, implementing sustainable warehousing practices offers opportunities for cost savings, improved efficiency, and positive brand reputation. This chapter explores methods to reduce waste and environmental impact, design energy-efficient warehouses, incorporate sustainable packaging, and learn from real-world examples of green warehousing in these industries.

9.1 Reducing Waste and Environmental Impact in Warehouses

Reducing waste is fundamental to sustainable warehousing. In automotive and manufacturing, where warehouses manage large volumes of materials and parts, optimizing waste management can minimize landfill contributions and improve operational efficiency.

Waste Reduction through Lean Principles

Lean warehousing, a principle that emphasizes waste elimination, can significantly improve sustainability. Techniques like 5S (Sort, Set in Order, Shine, Standardize, Sustain) and Kaizen (continuous improvement) reduce unnecessary movement, overstocking, and inefficient processes. These methods decrease waste by ensuring that materials and resources are only used as needed and continuously assessing areas for improvement.

Implementing Recycling Programs

Warehouses can recycle materials like cardboard, plastic, and metal scraps. Setting up recycling stations at key points encourages employees to separate waste properly, which not only reduces landfill but also allows valuable materials to be reprocessed. Many warehouses partner with waste management companies to streamline recycling and composting for biodegradable materials.

Minimizing Packaging Waste

Packaging waste is a major concern in warehousing. By switching to reusable and recyclable packaging materials, such as biodegradable plastics or returnable packaging containers, warehouses can significantly reduce their environmental impact. Some companies also adopt "right-sizing" packaging, ensuring that containers fit products precisely to reduce excess material usage.

Reducing Emissions with Efficient Transportation and Logistics

Transportation within and around the warehouse can be optimized to minimize fuel use and emissions. Adopting electric vehicles (EVs) for internal transport, optimizing delivery routes, and consolidating shipments help reduce greenhouse gas emissions associated with logistics.

9.2 Energy-Efficient Warehouse Design and Lighting

Energy efficiency is a cornerstone of sustainable warehousing, particularly in facilities that operate around the clock. By optimizing warehouse design and utilizing energy-efficient technologies, warehouses can significantly lower their energy consumption and costs.

Green Building Design

Green building standards, such as LEED (Leadership in Energy and Environmental Design), offer guidelines for designing sustainable warehouses. Warehouses built according to these standards often feature improved insulation, natural lighting, and energy-efficient HVAC systems, reducing the need for artificial lighting and heating or cooling. Proper layout design can also shorten travel distances, minimizing energy use for material handling equipment.

Efficient Lighting Systems

Lighting is a major energy consumer in warehouses. Replacing traditional lighting with LED bulbs, which use up to 80% less energy, can result in substantial savings. Installing automated lighting controls, like motion sensors or smart lighting systems that adjust based on occupancy, ensures lights are only on when necessary, further cutting energy costs.

Solar Panels and Renewable Energy

Many warehouses are integrating solar panels on rooftops to generate renewable energy onsite. Solar energy reduces reliance on grid electricity and provides a sustainable source of power, often with a quick return on investment through energy savings. In some cases, excess energy can be sold back to the grid, creating an additional revenue stream.

Energy-Efficient HVAC Systems

Heating, ventilation, and air conditioning (HVAC) systems are crucial for maintaining optimal conditions in a warehouse but can be energy-intensive. High-efficiency HVAC systems, combined with energy management systems that regulate temperatures based on activity and time of day, can greatly reduce energy use and costs. Insulation improvements and air curtains in entryways can further enhance efficiency by minimizing energy loss.

9.3 Sustainable Packaging and Material Handling

Sustainable packaging and eco-friendly material handling practices are key components of green warehousing. In automotive and manufacturing, where large volumes of materials move through the warehouse, these practices have a notable environmental impact.

Reusable Packaging Solutions

Using reusable packaging, such as crates, pallets, and containers, reduces waste and lowers long-term packaging costs. For instance, durable plastic or metal containers can be used repeatedly, replacing disposable alternatives like cardboard boxes. Some warehouses also use collapsible packaging that can be returned easily for reuse.

Eco-Friendly Materials

When reusable packaging isn't feasible, selecting recyclable or biodegradable materials, such as biodegradable bubble wrap or recycled paper, helps minimize environmental impact. Many companies in automotive and manufacturing have committed to using sustainable materials as part of their corporate social responsibility (CSR) strategies.

Optimizing Material Handling Equipment for Sustainability

Electrifying material handling equipment, such as forklifts and automated guided vehicles (AGVs), reduces emissions compared to diesel or gasoline-powered alternatives. Electric equipment is not only more energy-efficient but also produces no tailpipe emissions, which improves indoor air quality. Additionally, these vehicles often have longer lifespans and lower maintenance costs, providing long-term economic benefits.

Smart Packaging Solutions

Smart packaging technologies, like RFID tags, help reduce waste by improving inventory visibility and tracking expiration dates. This visibility minimizes the risk of spoilage and damage, ensuring materials and products are only moved or replaced as needed. Reducing the risk of damaged goods cuts down on waste, as fewer items need to be discarded or reprocessed.

9.4 Case Studies: Green Warehousing Practices in Automotive and Manufacturing

Examining successful examples of green warehousing in automotive and manufacturing can provide valuable insights and inspiration for companies seeking to adopt sustainable practices.

Case Study: Toyota's Eco-Friendly Warehousing

Toyota has long been a leader in green practices within automotive warehousing. The company has implemented energy-efficient lighting, solar power, and a robust recycling program in its distribution centers. By reusing packaging and employing efficient material handling systems, Toyota has reduced waste significantly while achieving high operational efficiency. The company's use of automated forklifts and AGVs has also lowered energy consumption and increased productivity.

Case Study: BMW's Sustainable Packaging Initiatives

BMW has prioritized sustainable packaging across its supply chain, particularly in its European manufacturing plants. The company employs reusable packaging containers and pallets, reducing its dependency on single-use plastics and cardboard. BMW also partners with suppliers to standardize packaging sizes and materials, enabling reuse and recycling on a large scale. This initiative has not only reduced waste but also cut packaging costs.

Case Study: Ford's Energy-Efficient Warehouses

Ford has implemented green building designs in its warehouses, featuring energy-efficient HVAC systems and LED lighting. Ford's facilities utilize renewable energy, including solar panels, and employ high-performance insulation to reduce heating and cooling costs. Additionally, the company has established strict energy management protocols, resulting in decreased overall energy consumption and enhanced environmental performance.

Case Study: General Motors' Zero Waste Strategy

General Motors (GM) has adopted a "zero-waste" approach in several of its warehousing and manufacturing sites, focusing on reusing, recycling, or converting waste materials into energy. GM achieves nearly 90% waste diversion in some facilities by meticulously separating waste, finding new uses for manufacturing by-products, and implementing closed-loop recycling systems. This approach not only reduces waste disposal costs but also aligns with GM's broader sustainability goals.

Adopting sustainable warehousing practices in automotive and manufacturing is essential for reducing environmental impact and improving operational efficiency. From reducing waste to implementing energy-efficient designs, these practices contribute to an eco-friendly and cost-effective warehouse operation. As demonstrated by companies like Toyota, BMW, Ford, and GM, investing in sustainable solutions not only benefits the environment but also enhances a company's reputation and supports long-term economic sustainability. By embracing these practices, warehouses in the automotive and manufacturing sectors can lead the way toward a more sustainable future.

Chapter 10: Warehouse Performance Metrics and KPIs

Warehouse performance metrics and key performance indicators (KPIs) are essential tools for measuring and optimizing operations. In automotive and manufacturing industries, where warehouses play a critical role in the supply chain, effective performance measurement drives efficiency, reduces costs, and ensures timely delivery of products. This chapter explores the most critical KPIs for warehouse operations, the role of data and analytics in performance improvement, methods for benchmarking, goal setting, and real-world case examples.

10.1 Key Performance Indicators for Warehouse Operations

KPIs provide a quantifiable measure of warehouse performance, enabling managers to identify inefficiencies, evaluate productivity, and make data-driven decisions. Below are the critical KPIs that warehouses in the automotive and manufacturing sectors typically monitor:

1. Order Accuracy

$$\text{Order Accuracy (\%)} = \left(\frac{\text{Total Accurate Orders}}{\text{Total Orders Shipped}} \right) \times 100$$

Importance: Accurate order fulfillment reduces returns, improves customer satisfaction, and enhances supply chain reliability. For example, a parts supplier in the automotive industry must ensure that the correct components are delivered to avoid production delays.

2. Inventory Accuracy

Definition: Compares recorded inventory to physical stock levels.

Formula:

$$\text{Inventory Accuracy (\%)} = \left(\frac{\text{Accurate Stock Count}}{\text{Total Stock Count}} \right) \times 100$$

Importance: Ensures stock records align with reality, minimizing shortages or overstock situations.

3. Order Cycle Time

Definition: Measures the time taken to process an order from receipt to shipment.

$$\text{Order Cycle Time} = \text{Order Shipment Time} - \text{Order Receipt Time}$$

Order Receipt Time

Order Cycle Time=Order Shipment Time−Order Receipt Time

Importance: Reducing order cycle time enhances customer satisfaction and improves overall efficiency.

4. Dock-to-Stock Time

Definition: Tracks the time taken to move items from receiving to storage.

Importance: Shorter dock-to-stock times improve inventory availability and reduce bottlenecks in inbound operations.

5. Picking Accuracy

Definition: Evaluates the accuracy of the picking process.

Formula:

$$\text{Picking Accuracy (\%)} = \left(\frac{\text{Accurate Picks}}{\text{Total Picks}} \right) \times 100$$

Importance: Incorrect picking leads to errors in order fulfillment, increased returns, and operational inefficiencies.

6. Space Utilization

Definition: Measures how effectively warehouse space is used.

Formula:

$$\text{Space Utilization (\%)} = \left(\frac{\text{Used Storage Area}}{\text{Total Storage Area}} \right) \times 100$$

Importance: Optimizing space reduces storage costs and maximizes the facility's capacity.

7. Labor Productivity

Definition: Tracks the output of warehouse staff in relation to tasks completed.

Formula:

$$\text{Labor Productivity} = \frac{\text{Tasks Completed}}{\text{Labor Hours Worked}}$$

Importance: Enhancing labor productivity reduces costs and ensures efficient resource utilization.

8. Shipping Accuracy

Definition: Measures the accuracy of shipped orders.

Importance: Accurate shipments reduce customer complaints and operational disruptions.

9. Return Rate

Definition: The percentage of orders returned due to errors or defects.

Formula:

$$\text{Return Rate } (\%) = \left(\frac{\text{Total Returns}}{\text{Total Orders Shipped}} \right) \times 100$$

Importance: High return rates signal issues in quality control, order accuracy, or packaging.

10.2 Using Data and Analytics to Improve Warehouse Efficiency

Incorporating data and analytics into warehouse operations is critical for identifying inefficiencies and making informed decisions. Technologies like IoT, AI, and advanced software platforms enable real-time data collection, analysis, and reporting.

1. Real-Time Tracking and Monitoring

Technologies: RFID, IoT sensors, and barcoding systems enable real-time inventory tracking.

Benefits: Provides accurate stock levels, prevents stockouts, and ensures quick replenishment.

Example: Automotive warehouses use RFID tags to track high-value components, reducing inventory loss and misplacement.

2. Predictive Analytics

Definition: Uses historical data to forecast demand, inventory needs, and potential disruptions.

Applications:

Forecasting seasonal demand to manage fluctuating inventory levels.

Predicting equipment maintenance needs to reduce downtime.

Example: Manufacturing warehouses use predictive analytics to plan inventory for production peaks, ensuring sufficient stock of raw materials.

3. Warehouse Management Systems (WMS)

Role: Centralizes data collection and integrates KPIs into dashboards for easy monitoring.

Features:

Performance analytics.

Automated reporting.

Integration with ERP systems.

Impact: Improves decision-making and operational visibility.

10.3 Benchmarking and Setting Goals for Continuous Improvement

Benchmarking involves comparing a warehouse's performance metrics against industry standards or competitors. It provides a framework for setting realistic goals and driving continuous improvement.

1. Internal Benchmarking

Definition: Compares performance across departments or facilities within the same organization.

Example: A manufacturing company compares order accuracy rates between regional warehouses to identify best practices.

2. External Benchmarking

Definition: Compares performance with competitors or industry standards.

Sources: Industry reports, trade associations, or third-party benchmarking services.

Example: Automotive warehouses benchmark their dock-to-stock times against competitors to stay competitive.

3. SMART Goals for Improvement

Specific: Clearly define the metric to improve (e.g., increase picking accuracy by 10%).

Measurable: Use quantifiable KPIs.

Achievable: Set realistic targets based on benchmarking data.

Relevant: Align goals with business objectives.

Time-Bound: Establish deadlines for achieving goals.

10.4 Case Examples: Metrics for Success in Automotive and Manufacturing Warehouses

1. Toyota: Excellence in Order Accuracy

Toyota's warehouses maintain an impressive 99.9% order accuracy rate by implementing lean warehousing principles, investing in advanced WMS, and regularly training staff. This high level of accuracy minimizes returns and strengthens the company's reputation for reliability.

2. BMW: Optimizing Space Utilization

BMW improved space utilization by 20% in its European warehouses by adopting vertical storage systems and automated storage and retrieval systems (AS/RS). These technologies maximize available space while reducing retrieval times.

3. Ford: Reducing Order Cycle Time

Ford optimized its order cycle time by integrating IoT sensors and AI-driven analytics. These technologies enable real-time tracking of orders, streamlining the process from order receipt to shipment. As a result, Ford reduced its average cycle time by 30%.

4. General Motors (GM): Improving Labor Productivity

GM focused on labor productivity by introducing collaborative robots ("cobots") in its warehouses. Cobots work alongside human workers to handle repetitive tasks, such as picking and packing, allowing employees to focus on value-added activities. This initiative boosted labor productivity by 25%.

5. Tesla: Leveraging Predictive Analytics

Tesla uses predictive analytics to manage inventory levels for its manufacturing plants. By analyzing demand patterns and production schedules, Tesla ensures optimal stock levels, reducing carrying costs while preventing stockouts.

Warehouse performance metrics and KPIs are indispensable for ensuring operational excellence in automotive and manufacturing industries. By tracking critical metrics like order accuracy, inventory accuracy, and labor productivity, warehouses can identify inefficiencies and implement targeted improvements. Leveraging data and analytics provides deeper insights, enabling predictive planning and real-time decision-making. Through benchmarking and goal-setting, warehouses can foster a culture of continuous improvement. The success stories of industry leaders like Toyota, BMW, and Tesla highlight the transformative impact of effective performance measurement, offering valuable lessons for warehouses striving to optimize their operations.

Chapter 11: Managing Returns and Reverse Logistics

Managing returns and reverse logistics is a critical aspect of warehouse management, especially in the automotive and manufacturing industries. Effective handling of returns and reverse logistics can minimize costs, recover value from returned goods, and support sustainability goals. This chapter explores the importance of returns management, the processes involved in reverse logistics, strategies for recycling and refurbishing, and the financial and operational impact of reverse logistics on warehouses.

11.1 Importance of Returns Management in Automotive and Manufacturing

Returns management, often overlooked in supply chain operations, plays a vital role in maintaining customer satisfaction, managing inventory, and promoting sustainability.

1. Customer Satisfaction and Retention

Significance: In the automotive and manufacturing sectors, ensuring timely and accurate handling of returns enhances customer loyalty.

Example: A manufacturer receiving faulty components from suppliers must replace or repair them swiftly to avoid production delays and maintain trust.

2. Regulatory Compliance

Relevance: Compliance with environmental and industry-specific regulations, such as disposing of hazardous materials, is critical.

Example: Automotive parts containing lead, batteries, or other hazardous substances must be returned and processed per legal requirements.

3. Financial Recovery

Opportunity: Efficient returns management recovers value through repair, refurbishment, or resale.

Example: A manufacturer may refurbish returned engines and sell them as certified pre-owned parts.

4. Sustainability and Circular Economy

Goal: By reusing, recycling, or refurbishing products, organizations contribute to a circular economy and reduce their environmental footprint.

Example: Automotive firms often recycle scrap metal from returned parts for reuse in manufacturing.

11.2 Reverse Logistics Processes for Faulty and Excess Inventory

Reverse logistics involves the movement of goods from customers or end-users back to the supply chain. It requires specialized processes to handle faulty, excess, or end-of-life inventory efficiently.

1. Key Stages in Reverse Logistics

Returns Authorization: Initiates the process by validating whether goods qualify for return.

Inspection and Sorting: Products are inspected for defects, categorized as reusable, repairable, or disposable.

Disposition: Decisions are made on whether to refurbish, recycle, resell, or dispose of items.

2. Faulty Inventory Handling

Process:

Faulty goods are returned to the warehouse.

Defective items are either repaired or sent to the original equipment manufacturer (OEM).

Quality checks ensure the product meets standards before reuse or resale.

Example: A returned engine part with a minor defect might be repaired and redeployed in the assembly line.

3. Excess Inventory Management

Challenge: Managing unsold or overproduced inventory without incurring significant losses.

Solution: Excess inventory can be redirected to secondary markets, used as spare parts, or recycled for raw materials.

Example: Manufacturing firms may redistribute surplus parts to aftermarket suppliers.

11.3 Recycling, Refurbishing, and Disposal Practices

Handling returned goods involves evaluating their potential for recycling, refurbishing, or disposal. These practices not only reduce costs but also align with environmental and sustainability goals.

1. Recycling

Process: Materials from returned goods are extracted and reprocessed into raw materials for manufacturing.

Application in Automotive:

Metals (aluminum, steel) from old parts are recycled into new components.

Plastic trims and covers are shredded and repurposed.

Benefits: Reduces waste and lowers costs by minimizing the need for virgin materials.

2. Refurbishing

Process: Returned items are repaired and restored to original working conditions.

Examples in Manufacturing:

Faulty machinery is repaired and redeployed.

Returned electronic control units (ECUs) are refurbished for resale.

Economic Impact: Refurbished goods provide a cost-effective alternative to new products while extending their lifecycle.

3. Disposal

Process: When recycling or refurbishing is not viable, items are disposed of responsibly.

Automotive Examples:

Hazardous materials like batteries are processed in compliance with regulations.

Non-recyclable waste is incinerated or sent to landfills as a last resort.

Considerations: Disposal methods must minimize environmental harm and comply with local regulations.

11.4 Cost and Impact of Reverse Logistics on Warehousing

Reverse logistics significantly impacts warehouse operations, influencing costs, efficiency, and overall supply chain effectiveness.

1. Cost Factors

Transportation Costs: Moving returned goods from customers to warehouses and processing centers.

Labor Costs: Increased workload for inspection, sorting, and repair activities.

Storage Costs: Storing returned items until their disposition is decided.

Technology Investments: Systems for tracking and managing returns, such as Warehouse Management Systems (WMS).

Example: A manufacturing firm may need additional labor and storage capacity during recall events, increasing operational costs.

2. Operational Challenges

Complexity of Processes: Reverse logistics involves more steps than traditional outbound logistics.

Space Constraints: Warehouses may need separate areas for returned goods, reducing space for regular inventory.

Quality Control: Ensuring that refurbished or recycled items meet stringent quality standards.

3. Financial Impact

Revenue Recovery: Effective reverse logistics recovers value by reselling refurbished goods or recycling materials.

Cost Savings: Recycling and reuse reduce raw material costs, while proper disposal minimizes penalties for non-compliance.

Example: Automotive firms that recycle scrap metal save significantly on raw material costs for manufacturing.

4. Environmental and Brand Impact

Sustainability Goals: Efficient reverse logistics aligns with corporate sustainability initiatives.

Customer Perception: Transparent and responsible handling of returns enhances brand reputation.

Example: A manufacturer implementing a take-back program for end-of-life vehicles may be viewed as an environmentally responsible brand.

Case Study: Reverse Logistics in the Automotive Industry

BMW's Recycling Initiatives

BMW has a comprehensive reverse logistics program that focuses on recycling and reusing materials. The company collects end-of-life vehicles and dismantles them to recover high-value materials such as aluminum, steel, and rare earth metals. This initiative has reduced raw material procurement costs and aligns with the company's sustainability goals.

Toyota's Circular Economy Approach

Toyota employs reverse logistics to refurbish and recycle returned parts. For instance, batteries from hybrid vehicles are collected, tested, and refurbished for resale or recycled for materials. This process not only supports Toyota's commitment to environmental responsibility but also generates additional revenue streams.

Ford's Return Management System

Ford has developed an advanced returns management system integrated with its Warehouse Management System (WMS). This system tracks returned parts, categorizes them for repair, resale, or recycling, and automates key processes to reduce handling time and costs. As a result, Ford has significantly improved the efficiency of its reverse logistics operations.

Returns management and reverse logistics are indispensable for optimizing warehouse operations in the automotive and manufacturing sectors. By focusing on effective processes for handling faulty and excess inventory, recycling and refurbishing practices, and minimizing disposal costs, organizations can recover value, reduce waste, and support sustainability goals. Although reverse logistics presents challenges, such as increased costs and operational complexity, adopting advanced technologies and sustainable practices can transform these challenges into opportunities for growth and innovation. Companies like BMW, Toyota, and Ford exemplify how strategic reverse logistics practices can enhance efficiency, reduce environmental impact, and improve profitability.

Chapter 12: Transportation and Logistics Integration

Transportation and logistics integration is critical in enhancing the efficiency of warehouse operations, especially in the automotive and manufacturing industries. Warehouses serve as the nexus between production, suppliers, and end customers. Effective coordination between transportation and warehousing minimizes lead times, reduces costs, and ensures a seamless flow of goods across the supply chain. This chapter examines the role of warehouses in the broader supply chain, strategies for integrating logistics, and techniques to optimize transportation specific to the automotive and manufacturing sectors.

12.1 Role of Warehouses in the Broader Supply Chain

Warehouses are essential hubs in the supply chain, bridging the gap between production and consumption. Their role extends beyond storage to include value-added services, which optimize supply chain efficiency.

1. Facilitating Inventory Management

Storage Functions: Warehouses hold raw materials, work-in-progress (WIP), and finished goods until they are needed.

Buffer Stock: Warehouses serve as buffers against supply chain disruptions, ensuring continuity in production and distribution.

Example: Automotive warehouses store critical components such as engines and transmissions to prevent production halts.

2. Supporting Just-in-Time (JIT) Operations

Significance: In JIT systems, warehouses ensure timely delivery of materials to production lines to minimize excess inventory.

Example: A warehouse near an automotive assembly plant delivers parts directly to the production line within specified time windows.

3. Enabling Distribution

Hub Functionality: Warehouses act as central distribution points, consolidating goods from multiple suppliers and distributing them to customers.

Example: A regional distribution center for a manufacturing firm consolidates parts from suppliers and distributes finished products to dealers.

4. Value-Added Services

Customization: Warehouses handle activities like packaging, labeling, and assembly, which add value to goods before shipping.

Example: An automotive warehouse installs software in electronic control units (ECUs) before dispatching them to OEMs.

12.2 Coordination with Logistics for Seamless Inbound and Outbound

Effective logistics coordination ensures smooth inbound flow of raw materials and components, as well as efficient outbound distribution of finished goods.

1. Inbound Logistics Coordination

Supplier Collaboration: Real-time communication with suppliers ensures timely delivery of materials.

Cross-Docking: Reduces handling time by transferring materials directly from inbound to outbound transportation.

Example: A manufacturing warehouse receives components from suppliers and immediately routes them to assembly lines without extended storage.

2. Outbound Logistics Coordination

Route Optimization: Planning efficient delivery routes reduces transportation costs and delivery times.

Order Fulfillment: Warehouses coordinate with logistics providers to ensure accurate and timely order delivery.

Example: An automotive parts warehouse ships orders to dealerships using optimized delivery schedules to reduce fuel costs.

3. Integration Through Technology

Use of WMS and TMS: Integrating Warehouse Management Systems (WMS) with Transportation Management Systems (TMS) enhances visibility and control.

Example: Real-time tracking of shipments enables warehouses to prepare for incoming goods and dispatch outbound loads promptly.

4. Collaborative Planning

Joint Decision-Making: Warehouses and logistics providers collaborate on demand forecasting, inventory planning, and transportation schedules.

Example: A warehouse collaborates with a third-party logistics (3PL) provider to synchronize inventory levels with transportation availability.

12.3 Managing Transportation Needs Specific to Automotive and Manufacturing

Transportation needs in the automotive and manufacturing sectors are unique due to the nature of goods, production schedules, and supply chain complexity.

1. Handling Large and Specialized Goods

Challenge: Transporting oversized items such as engines or machinery requires specialized equipment and logistics.

Solution: Use flatbed trucks, cranes, or modular transport systems for safe and efficient handling.

Example: Shipping large automotive molds to assembly plants.

2. Managing Time-Sensitive Deliveries

Requirement: Timely delivery of materials is critical to avoid production delays.

Solution: Use expedited shipping methods, such as air freight or dedicated trucking.

Example: Delivering just-in-sequence (JIS) parts to an automotive assembly line.

3. Ensuring Product Safety and Compliance

Concern: Transporting delicate or hazardous materials, such as batteries or chemicals, requires adherence to safety regulations.

Solution: Use specialized packaging, temperature control systems, and compliance with international transportation standards.

Example: Shipping lithium-ion batteries for electric vehicles in compliance with UN38.3 regulations.

4. Managing Multi-Modal Transportation

Complexity: Combining rail, road, sea, and air transport requires precise coordination.

Solution: Use intermodal containers and integrated logistics systems.

Example: Exporting automotive components to overseas markets using a combination of sea and rail transport.

12.4 Reducing Lead Times and Costs Through Logistics-Warehouse Integration

Integration between logistics and warehousing improves efficiency, reduces operational costs, and enhances customer satisfaction by minimizing lead times.

1. Streamlining Processes

Cross-Docking: Eliminates unnecessary storage by transferring goods directly from inbound to outbound transportation.

Example: A warehouse cross-docks incoming tires from suppliers to outgoing shipments for assembly plants.

2. Leveraging Advanced Analytics

Predictive Analytics: Forecasting demand and transportation needs reduces delays and overstocking.

Example: Using analytics to predict peak demand for manufacturing parts and adjusting logistics accordingly.

3. Reducing Idle Times

Real-Time Scheduling: Dynamic scheduling minimizes wait times for loading and unloading at warehouses.

Example: A TMS coordinates truck arrivals with warehouse loading docks to reduce idle time.

4. Collaborative Transportation Management

Shared Resources: Partnering with other firms to share transportation resources reduces costs.

Example: Multiple automotive firms share transportation services for non-competing routes to maximize truck utilization.

5. Implementing Sustainable Practices

Eco-Friendly Logistics: Using electric vehicles, optimizing routes, and consolidating shipments reduces environmental impact and costs.

Example: An automotive firm uses electric trucks for local deliveries to reduce carbon emissions.

Case Examples: Logistics-Warehouse Integration in Automotive and Manufacturing

1. Tesla's Gigafactories

Tesla's Gigafactories integrate production, warehousing, and logistics under one roof. Raw materials are received just-in-time, and finished batteries are dispatched directly to assembly plants. This integration reduces transportation costs and lead times, while streamlining inventory management.

2. BMW's Logistics Network

BMW employs a global logistics network integrated with its warehouses to ensure efficient inbound and outbound transportation. The use of technology, such as RFID tracking and automated loading systems, enhances visibility and reduces lead times.

3. Toyota's Just-In-Time Logistics

Toyota's warehousing and logistics operate on a JIT model, with parts delivered directly to production lines. This minimizes storage requirements and ensures efficient use of transportation resources.

Transportation and logistics integration is essential for efficient warehouse operations in the automotive and manufacturing industries. By coordinating inbound and outbound logistics, managing unique transportation needs, and leveraging technology, organizations can reduce lead times and operational costs. Advanced strategies such as cross-docking, predictive analytics, and collaborative transportation management further enhance efficiency. Real-world examples from Tesla, BMW, and Toyota highlight the transformative potential of seamless logistics-warehouse integration, demonstrating its impact on supply chain performance and competitiveness.

Chapter 13: Best Practices in Automotive and Manufacturing Warehousing

Automotive and manufacturing industries demand warehousing operations that are highly efficient, cost-effective, and adaptable to dynamic market conditions. Implementing best practices allows warehouses to achieve these objectives while maintaining high standards of quality and reliability. This chapter delves into proven strategies for successful warehousing, examines lessons from leading companies, and offers practical tips for adopting best practices tailored to the automotive and manufacturing sectors.

13.1 Case Studies of Successful Warehousing Strategies

1. Toyota: Mastering Just-in-Time (JIT) Warehousing

Background: Toyota pioneered the Just-in-Time (JIT) system, which emphasizes delivering the right materials at the right time to minimize inventory holding.

Warehouse Strategy:

Smaller, strategically located warehouses near manufacturing plants.

Use of Kanban systems for real-time inventory replenishment.

High reliance on supplier collaboration and logistics integration.

Outcome: Drastic reduction in inventory costs and increased production efficiency.

2. Tesla: Automation and Vertical Integration

Background: Tesla's Gigafactories integrate manufacturing, warehousing, and logistics into a unified operation.

Warehouse Strategy:

Automated storage and retrieval systems (AS/RS) to manage components like battery cells.

Direct integration of production lines and warehouses under one roof.

Extensive use of robotics for material handling and inventory management.

Outcome: Enhanced operational efficiency, reduced transportation costs, and streamlined production.

3. BMW: Leveraging Data-Driven Operations

Background: BMW focuses on data analytics to optimize warehousing and logistics across its global supply chain.

Warehouse Strategy:

RFID-based tracking for real-time visibility of inventory.

Automated systems for order picking and packing.

Predictive analytics to forecast demand and adjust inventory levels.

Outcome: Reduced lead times, improved order accuracy, and higher customer satisfaction.

13.2 Best Practices for Enhancing Efficiency and Reducing Costs

1. Optimize Warehouse Layout and Design

Principle: Maximize space utilization and streamline workflows.

Tactics:

Use vertical storage solutions such as high-bay racking systems.

Implement flexible layouts that can adapt to changes in inventory volumes.

Create dedicated zones for raw materials, WIP, and finished goods.

Benefits: Improved productivity and reduced handling time.

2. Embrace Lean Warehousing Principles

Principle: Minimize waste in warehouse operations.

Tactics:

Identify and eliminate non-value-adding activities such as redundant handling.

Implement 5S methodology to maintain an organized and efficient workspace.

Use Value Stream Mapping (VSM) to identify process bottlenecks.

Benefits: Reduced operational costs and increased efficiency.

3. Leverage Advanced Technology

Principle: Integrate cutting-edge technology to improve warehouse operations.

Tactics:

Deploy Warehouse Management Systems (WMS) for better inventory control.

Use IoT-enabled sensors for real-time monitoring of storage conditions.

Invest in robotics and automation for material handling.

Benefits: Enhanced accuracy, faster operations, and reduced labor costs.

4. Prioritize Workforce Training and Development

Principle: Equip employees with the skills needed for modern warehousing.

Tactics:

Conduct regular training sessions on new technologies and safety protocols.

Empower staff with cross-functional roles to improve adaptability.

Establish incentive programs to boost morale and retention.

Benefits: Higher workforce productivity and reduced turnover rates.

5. Adopt Sustainable Practices

Principle: Minimize the environmental impact of warehousing activities.

Tactics:

Use energy-efficient lighting and HVAC systems.

Reduce packaging waste through reusable materials.

Optimize transportation routes to lower carbon emissions.

Benefits: Cost savings and improved corporate sustainability.

13.3 Lessons from Leading Automotive and Manufacturing Companies

1. Flexibility is Key

Lesson: Warehouses must be agile to adapt to fluctuations in demand.

Example: Ford's global warehouse network uses modular designs to accommodate changing inventory needs.

2. Invest in Technology

Lesson: Advanced technologies provide a competitive edge in efficiency and accuracy.

Example: General Motors employs AI-driven analytics to forecast inventory requirements and avoid stockouts.

3. Collaboration Across the Supply Chain

Lesson: Strong relationships with suppliers and logistics partners enhance operational efficiency.

Example: Bosch integrates its warehouses with supplier systems to enable seamless inventory replenishment.

4. Quality Control is Non-Negotiable

Lesson: Maintaining high-quality standards prevents downstream disruptions.

Example: Mercedes-Benz warehouses conduct rigorous inspections of incoming materials to ensure compliance with production standards.

13.4 Practical Tips for Implementing Best Practices in Warehousing

1. Conduct Regular Audits

Tip: Perform routine assessments to identify inefficiencies and areas for improvement.

Implementation: Use third-party auditors or internal teams to evaluate storage conditions, workflow, and inventory accuracy.

2. Standardize Processes

Tip: Create standard operating procedures (SOPs) for key warehouse tasks.

Implementation: Document best practices for receiving, put-away, picking, and shipping processes.

3. Use Data to Drive Decisions

Tip: Leverage analytics to monitor performance metrics and identify trends.

Implementation: Track KPIs such as order accuracy, pick rates, and cycle times to guide continuous improvement.

4. Focus on Scalability

Tip: Plan for future growth when designing warehouse operations.

Implementation: Choose scalable technologies and layouts that can accommodate increased volumes.

5. Engage Employees in Continuous Improvement

Tip: Encourage staff to participate in identifying inefficiencies and proposing solutions.

Implementation: Establish suggestion boxes, feedback sessions, and recognition programs.

By adopting best practices, automotive and manufacturing warehouses can significantly enhance their operational efficiency, reduce costs, and deliver greater value across the supply chain. Lessons from industry leaders like Toyota, Tesla, and BMW emphasize the importance of technology, sustainability, and collaboration. Practical tips, such as conducting audits, standardizing processes, and engaging employees, provide actionable insights for continuous improvement. As the warehousing landscape evolves, staying ahead requires commitment to innovation and a relentless focus on excellence.

Chapter 14: The Future of Warehousing in Automotive and Manufacturing Industries

As technology and innovation continue to reshape the global supply chain, warehousing within the automotive and manufacturing industries is entering a transformative phase. From autonomous vehicles to blockchain, the future of warehousing promises greater efficiency, cost-effectiveness, and sustainability. This chapter explores emerging technologies, the integration of autonomous systems, the challenges and opportunities of digital transformation, and the evolving roles of the future workforce.

14.1 Emerging Technologies and Trends

1. Blockchain for Supply Chain Transparency

What It Is: Blockchain offers an immutable ledger to track goods across the supply chain.

Applications in Warehousing:

Traceability: Ensures authenticity and compliance for automotive parts.

Inventory Management: Provides real-time updates and reduces errors in record-keeping.

Collaboration: Enhances trust among stakeholders, including suppliers, manufacturers, and logistics providers.

Example: BMW uses blockchain to verify ethically sourced cobalt for electric vehicle batteries.

2. Artificial Intelligence (AI)

What It Is: AI analyzes complex datasets to optimize operations.

Applications in Warehousing:

Predictive Analytics: Forecast demand fluctuations to maintain optimal inventory levels.

Route Optimization: Enhances the efficiency of pick-and-pack operations.

Fault Detection: Identifies defective products early in the supply chain.

Example: Tesla's Gigafactories leverage AI-driven systems to manage inventory and streamline production.

3. Predictive Analytics

What It Is: Predictive analytics uses historical data to forecast future trends.

Applications in Warehousing:

Demand Planning: Predicts inventory needs based on market trends.

Maintenance Scheduling: Anticipates equipment failures, reducing downtime.

Supply Chain Resilience: Identifies vulnerabilities and mitigates risks proactively.

4. Internet of Things (IoT)

What It Is: IoT enables interconnected devices to share data in real-time.

Applications in Warehousing:

Smart Shelves: Monitor stock levels and send automated restocking alerts.

Temperature Sensors: Ensure optimal conditions for sensitive automotive components.

Asset Tracking: Provides visibility into the location of high-value items.

14.2 The Role of Autonomous Vehicles and Drones in Warehousing

1. Autonomous Mobile Robots (AMRs)

Function: AMRs navigate warehouse floors using sensors and AI.

Applications:

Order Picking: Reduces the need for manual labor.

Material Transport: Moves heavy loads efficiently.

Inventory Checks: Scans barcodes and RFID tags for real-time accuracy.

Example: Amazon's use of Kiva robots has revolutionized e-commerce warehousing.

2. Drones

Function: Drones offer aerial capabilities for quick and efficient tasks.

Applications:

Inventory Audits: Fly through aisles to count inventory.

Surveillance: Enhance security by monitoring large facilities.

Last-Mile Delivery: Expedite the transportation of small, high-priority items.

Example: DHL employs drones in remote locations for urgent deliveries.

3. Autonomous Forklifts and AGVs

Function: Autonomous Guided Vehicles (AGVs) replace traditional forklifts.

Applications:

Pallet Transport: Safely moves pallets across the warehouse.

Loading/Unloading: Automates truck-to-warehouse transfers.

Hazard Mitigation: Reduces accidents by following predefined routes.

Example: BMW's facilities use AGVs for efficient material handling.

14.3 Preparing for Digital Transformation in Warehousing

1. Challenges of Digital Transformation

High Implementation Costs: Initial investments in technology can be significant.

Integration Complexity: Ensuring seamless communication between legacy systems and new technologies.

Workforce Resistance: Employees may fear job displacement or struggle with adopting new tools.

2. Steps to Successful Digital Transformation

Develop a Clear Roadmap: Outline objectives, timelines, and milestones for digitization.

Invest in Scalable Technologies: Choose solutions that can adapt to future needs.

Foster a Culture of Innovation: Encourage employees to embrace change and suggest improvements.

Collaborate with Technology Providers: Partner with experts for smooth implementation.

3. Benefits of Digital Transformation

Increased Efficiency: Automation reduces human error and accelerates processes.

Enhanced Decision-Making: Data-driven insights lead to better operational strategies.

Improved Customer Satisfaction: Faster order fulfillment and accurate deliveries enhance the customer experience.

14.4 The Future Workforce: Skills and Roles in the Modern Warehouse

1. Evolving Roles in Warehousing

Automation Specialists: Operate and maintain robots and automated systems.

Data Analysts: Interpret warehouse data to identify trends and optimize operations.

IoT Technicians: Manage interconnected devices and sensors.

Cybersecurity Experts: Protect warehouse systems from digital threats.

2. Skills for the Future Workforce

Technical Proficiency: Familiarity with WMS, robotics, and IoT platforms.

Data Literacy: Ability to analyze and utilize data for decision-making.

Adaptability: Flexibility to learn new technologies and processes.

Problem-Solving: Capacity to troubleshoot and resolve operational issues quickly.

3. Workforce Development Strategies

Training Programs: Offer courses on advanced technologies and safety practices.

Apprenticeships: Partner with educational institutions to build a talent pipeline.

Upskilling Initiatives: Provide existing employees with opportunities to learn new skills.

Employee Engagement: Foster a sense of ownership and pride in warehouse roles.

The future of warehousing in the automotive and manufacturing industries is one of unprecedented innovation and transformation. Emerging technologies like blockchain, AI, and IoT are set to revolutionize traditional operations, while autonomous vehicles and drones promise unparalleled efficiency. However, the transition to digital warehousing requires careful planning, investment, and a commitment to workforce development. By embracing these changes and preparing for the future, warehouses can position themselves as critical enablers of supply chain excellence.

www.ingramcontent.com/pod-product-compliance
Lightning Source LLC
Chambersburg PA
CBHW071518220526

45472CB00003B/1060